Butterflies In My Mind

Deepti Jethani

BookLeaf Publishing

India | USA | UK

Presentation by *BookLeaf Publishing*

Web: www.bookleafpub.com

E-mail: info@bookleafpub.com

ISBN: 9789363314641

First edition 2024

PREFACE

"Butterflies in My Mind" is a deeply personal journey into the realms of mental health and human emotion. Each poem is a reflection of my own encounters with anxiety, despair, hope, and healing. The delicate flutter of a butterfly, with its unpredictable and restless nature, serves as a metaphor for the undercurrent of tumultuous thoughts and feelings that define our inner worlds.

In crafting this collection, I was inspired by the introspective brilliance of Virginia Woolf, the evocative simplicity of Emily Dickinson, and the redemptive themes of Mary Oliver. Their works have profoundly influenced my understanding and articulation of the complex emotional landscapes we traverse.

The poems are organised into sections that mirror the stages of confronting mental health challenges: realisation, daily struggles, seeking help, and acceptance. It is my hope that these verses offer you solace, provoke thought, and foster a sense of connection, reminding you that you are not alone in your experiences.

Thank you for joining me on this intimate journey.

With gratitude,
Deepti.

TABLE OF CONTENTS

A Clockwork Toy	1
Instability	3
Stand-up Thoughts - I	5
Hey, Cutie!	7
Humble '90s Pies	9
Confrontation	11
Body Dysmorphia	13
Good Night	15
People & Places	17
Emotional Apparatus	19
Trauma	21
Catharsis-I	23
Catharsis-II	25
Matrimony	27
Religion	29
Child of Mediocrity	31
Problem of Plenty	33
Ode to Anxiety	35
Holding On	37
Grace	39
Freedom	41
Finding You	43
Chan Kitthan	45
Words	47
Abandonment	49
Burnt Oakwood	51
Old Man in the Woods	53
Reclamation	55
Sound of Death	57
Acknowledgements	58

A Clockwork Toy

My days bleed into each other, separated by a
few hours of punctuation.
Sleep spills over the afternoon like morning tea.

The sun sprawls itself from my window and
blinds my eyes.
I locate the small metal key jammed in the soft
arch of my back and tighten it like a screw:

It's done, I release.

The lights in the office are too loud.
I take my eyes out and put them in my drawer
for the day;
they rest while I work on the screen brainlessly.

Words and numbers are just small dots floating
over the screen.
"You just have to find the pattern," I say, but
they keep melting into each other:

I separate them.

The sounds are cutting the thin veil around me:
the printer, the coffee machine, the chatter of
colleagues.

I spend my breaks in the old cafeteria, my
deserted island. It's a break, really.

"Is it dark outside?"
I lose the sense of day and night every day.

I step outside—from my office and personality.
"Why is it still too bright?"
I jump in an auto and pat my bag:

I forget the eyes once again.
I don't need them though; I am still wound up.
My body moves mechanically.

Morning unspools and the alarm blares again.
But the key seems to be jammed tighter than
yesterday, again.

Instability

The tectonic plates beneath my emotional
landscape are always shifting,
overlapping, sometimes.

The light-reflecting glass walls in my office
curlicue and spiral closer every day.

I enter in and out of the ziplock bags of cities,
pretend to fasten them by interlocking their steel
grooves and mountain ridges.

I move from friend to friend like Hermit Crabs
moves shell to shell,
trying everything from underage exoskeletons to
smooth and pearly conches to beer cans.

The mud in my kutcha house is always
cascading from the walls,
ankles melting into soft sand.

Relationships are revolving doors made of pretty
men with scented shirts and musky bodies.

Life composed of soapsuds, bubbles in paint,
acrylic nails, condensation on glass windows.
I live in ephemeralities.

How does one even define home?
A person, place, animal, or thing?

Stand-up Thoughts - I

Polyamorous relationships are like dating on
steroids,
where multiple hearts intertwine, in a web of
affection—a factoid.

It's like running a multi-level marketing scheme
of dating;
we're the Oriflames of the scene, hearts
ever-rotating.

Ever heard of "More the merrier" believers?
Well, that's us, Modern Love's vast receivers.

It's not my fault, this dating concept I adore;
as a woman, I'm accustomed to variety, craving
more.

My bra comes in 37 designs in the market:
Half of us don't know how to wear half of them,
and more than half of the guys don't know how
to remove.
So, who's actually supporting bras? It's time to
move.

Hashtag 'Free the Nipple,' social messaging
profound.
But, I think I should steer clear of the superficial
ground.

As I ponder the crazy things I might one day say,
perhaps, on the day when the world folds itself
away.

And folds itself again, for the edges weren't
clean,
much like the edges of my lips, a bold lipliner's
sheen.

Ten minutes spent fixing what's not quite right,
after eight on red lipstick, painting the night.

Hey, Cutie!

She has opened several wounds of the past—the shabbily covered, hastily band-aided ones—and drained the old blood out to paint her lips.

The glint in her eyes is the ember of midnights she has burned over the years, alone, to keep herself warm.

The blackness in her hair is the several untamed serpents of societal pressures, braided neatly and decorated with a flower-shaped clip.

The crimson on her cheeks is the rosacea she developed while fighting too hard with the sun, every day.

Her body has borne gallons of blood loss mixed with uterine linings and, yet, stands tall.

And you think you have anything more to add to her beauty? How cute!

Humble '90s Pies

Mom never stored buttons, bobbins, or thimbles
in transparent plastics of Amul Butterscotch,
These tiny treasures and tchotchkes hid normally
in the small compartment of our rust-smelling,
dust-catching sewing machine.

Our evenings were made of tummy rumblings
for 5 Rs packets of Maggi and 10 Rs ki tamarind
chutney laced bhels.

Hide & Seek, GTA San Andreas, High School
Musical, coaching classes, McDonalds, acrylic
paints—
Words from the language of posh that we did not
speak.

Ours were clothes cinched by stitches on the
sides,
Super Mario Bros,
Tekken-3 in dimly lit game parlours,

packets of Natkhats,
saccharine-filled ice sticks,
evening strolls to a dusty playground with silted
slides.

When your childhood is not eyes fixated on tiny
screens of brick games,
synchronised dance movements or story-reading
sessions in summer classes,
It's a throw of the rugged, mud-covered plastic
ball from ground
to ground
to home
to ground,
and again.

Confrontation

…with God.

Why fix?
Let me carry the pieces with me, the carcasses of
my dreams,
With the belief that someday an elixir will be
found
To blow the breath,
So that they can at least look green,
Reminding me of my woes.

Else, the birds can feed,
Hope: some of them could reach with my piece
in beak,

For these are so bitter to eat,
And my beat can be felt, my soul can be seen.

Wish: some of them could make it there before
those pieces dry,
The ooze can be felt, the bleed can be seen,
Not with the belief to aid me indeed,
No mercy I need.

Oh, wings, just drop the shatters there, so you
can see,
Those parts of me filled with pride, parts of me
profane to hide.

Just keep these, thou,
For one day I will knock the door,
I will take those pieces back, not to mend, still
not to fix,
To burn them into ashes instead,
The demons I carried, then will be freed!
For then I will be filled and there will be no
pieces with me.

Dressed in my own wings, sun setting on my
sill,
shining from inside out, for I am with thee now.

Body Dysmorphia

"I can't do this," said I, hunched over the wash
basin,
"It's too much, I can't bear to face it, the pain."
With clenched hands and a heavy heart, I
counted down
from twenty to one, a slow and steady sound.

Standing straight, eyes still closed, afraid to see,
the monster staring back, the mirror, the key.
With fists clenched tight, I counted once more:
five, four, three, two, one, I opened the door.

Slowly, cautiously, I let my gaze roam,
from the legs, covered in fur, a deep brown tone.
Up to the belly, rough and matted, a sight,
then to the face, shapeless, barely human in
light.

The higher my gaze, the more ghastly the form:
a shapeless mass, covered in pus and storm.
A volcanic eruption, flesh and skin, all torn,
covered in molten lava, a nightmare born.

Horror and pity, emotions intertwined—
no one can endure this, it's beyond the mind.
Something must have happened, beyond
comprehension,
to create this monster, a soul in detention.

Good Night

What are you dreaming about these nights?

Is it still about you giving an exam in your old classroom settings, and the bell rings, and you run out of time?

Is it about you missing your alarm and jolting up from your sleep, all sweating and looking at your clock because you are late for work again?

Is it about a faceless monster chasing you in the middle of nowhere, and you try to scream your lungs out but no one can hear your cries?

Is it about you hanging from a cliff, barely holding on to the edge, and you are about to fall but can't scream as your voice freezes in your throat?

Is it about you getting bit by a snake that came out of nowhere and buried its teeth in the flesh of your ankle, and you are writhing in pain?

Is it about someone trying to choke you in your sleep, as their hands grip slowly but tightly around your neck until you run out of breath, and you still can't figure out their face?

Or, is it about a spirit standing at your bedside in the very room in which you are sleeping now, coming closer to you in slow motion, but you can't help because your body is just frozen?

Which is it tonight?

People & Places

I wonder how we separate places from people.

Others look for people in places,
I have been looking for places in people my
entire life:

some were cherry blossom gardens of Japan,

some were snow-sprinkled maple trees of
Canada,

some were roadside Turkish sheesh kebabs,

some late-night Brazilian clubs,

some were Aurora Borealis,

and some were just empty highways to remote cities.

I guess, this is what they mean when they say "You mean the world to me."

Emotional Apparatus

My emotional apparatus is all over the place. I remember sobbing over a lost feeding bottle just a year before this.
(Yes, I used to drink milk from a feeding bottle till I was 8.)

Or, the time I got a fever because I was crying the whole night,
when someone broke my favourite flower vase:
It was a toy made from cheap transparent plastic, with fake flowers painted on the insides of it. (It was not even that pretty.)

But did I cry when I saw my grandmother's dead body?

Who died almost as suddenly as you see a
gazelle dying in a Savannah on National
Geographic,
except there was no David Attenborough voice
to soothe you.

No, she was not chased by a lion or dangerous
carnivore,
or the man of the family in a patriarchal society,
as you call it.
She just died very suddenly when she slipped on
the floor,
while brushing her teeth in the morning. (A very
painless and peaceful death.)

And, she somehow knew she was going to die,
as she always talked about it.
She was awfully at peace with it,
like a gazelle who knew he is going to be hunted
down any second,
and, still, peacefully goes about his day.

So, like every other situation,
I just stood there where my mother was lying,
completely submerged in the ocean of my own
thoughts.

"Just a concussion." They said later on.

Trauma

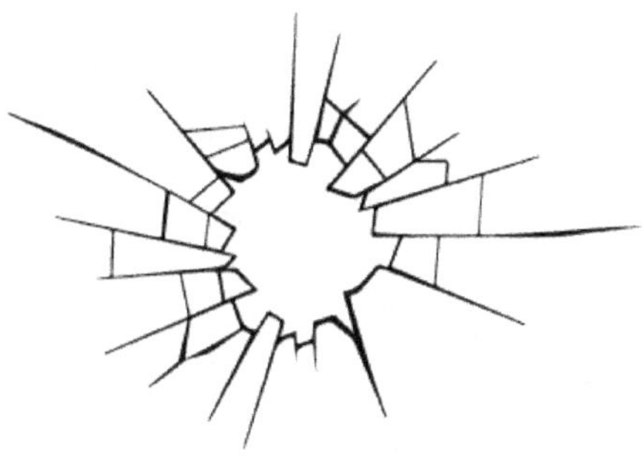

Trauma deftly carves a slender incision in the
skin with a heated blade,
an aperture into a world steeped in longing.

It burrows in the flesh and absorbs every drop of
light,
makes plastic fireflies with radiant bellies, stores
the remaining luminescence for future use.

It syphons the marrow of hope from the bones,
rendering them dry and brittle;
bones fated to fracture, not in a singular snap,
but under the persistent weight of time.

One by one, they splinter,
lacerating the veins, sinews, and muscles.

It is the agony of a thousand small deaths
preceding the final one.

You are not meant to bleed dry in an instant.

Catharsis-I

"And, how do you feel today?"

How do you unfurl your tongue
in a way that softens the description
of a time that felt like a razor blade
cutting through the soft clouds of young dreams;

when your entire childhood felt like a paper bag
around your head,

where the houses (yes, plural) you grew up in
were boxes of tin to hold your muffled screams;

the walls were always damp as sadness seeped
through them,
leaving water stains of monstrous shapes;

where you didn't really make paper planes from
the torn pages
but crumpled them up to stuff your hungry
mouths;

and going to school was like coming out of the
water gasping for air to breathe,
water with a brewing undercurrent constantly
churning your body;
outside air was equally putrid and damp,
laden with the smell of the rotting sea.

Catharsis-II

But each time I revisit the mausoleum of
memories (for the umpteenth time now),
the stench fades away a bit, like smoke coming
out of a distant house,

and the embers turn into ashes that render the
sky powdered grey.

For time has slowly unbraided the seaweeds
of the dark oceans wreathed in my hair.

And I have learned to weave all the threads of
bitterness into words—
a tapestry leading to the future.

And my parents are old now,
their skin shrivelled up like raisins;

Their soft bones and wrinkles are contour lines
of the emotional distance they have travelled
with time, with me.

And the waves of forgiveness have mattified the
rough stones
and whittled them into tiny, oval-shaped stones
which don't cut through my fingers anymore.

"I feel much better these days." I said as I eased
myself into the chair in the therapist's office.

Matrimony

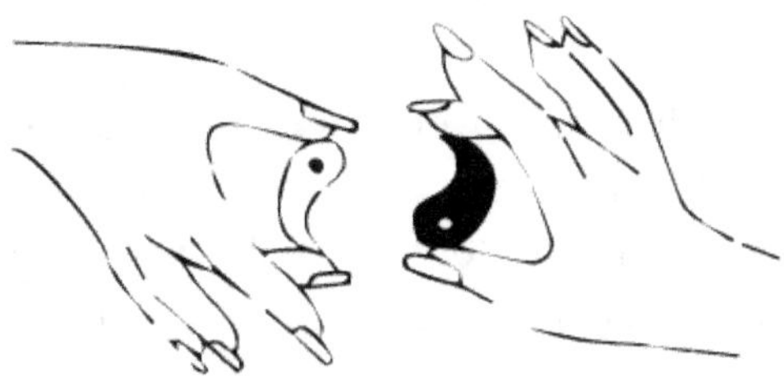

"Till death do us part."

But what if it doesn't, and we do?

You see, it's not just between you and me.
It's a weird concoction of two families, peppered
with rituals and societal beliefs.

And what if it crumbles under the weight of
it—the series of shared responsibilities and the
constant standing up to it?

You know wind stress over an extended period
can even split the seas
—Google Keywords: Scientific Explanation,
Moses, Red Sea.

In this world of almosts, where pretty Tinder
dates are just a "Ssup" away. (Not even a
"What's up," I am telling ya.)

And, my head is in Koh Samui and Nusa Penida,
Face in South Korea,
Limbs tracing the Northern Lights in different
countries. (They are just popping up everywhere
these days.)

How do you expect me to hold down and sit in
the hushes of old rituals that bind you and me till
eternity?
How do you expect a bond so encumbered by
the weight of "Happily Ever After" to last?

I just can't see.

Religion

My religious views are basically an assorted platter of different religions:

I prefer sajdah in a dargah any day: I want to tie dhaaga on the Jannati Darwaza crossing the ittar-scented lanes, offer mannat ki chaadar on the maqbara, and carry aqeedat ke phool.

I want to wear a white gown on my wedding day and kiss my groom: Someone playing harp in the background, I carry a bouquet of lush, pink flowers, and walk the aisle with my white gown sweeping the floor behind me.

I want to have a Bar mitzvah when my kid
enters his teens: My boy puts on a tefillin and
reads from the torah, the rabbi gives a talk while
we have a celebratory feast.

When I die, I want to be a vulture's feast at a
dakhma:
My body will lie on the gratings in the Tower of
Silence, vultures plucking the flesh and sinew
clean, and finally, my bones falling in the pit, to
be claimed by the ground.

In the end, I want people to mourn for exactly
twelve days after my death: They will have a
teeye ki rasam on the third day, women will do a
paath every evening, and people will have a
feast remembering me on the final day.

Child of Mediocrity

I know people who learned to live as a coiled-up
version of themselves,
like little snails inching whatever earth they
think they belong to;
their soft bodies trudging through the potted soil
in a ceramic concave, not in coarse woody
debris or juicy leaf litter on a forest floor.

The girl who quietly slithered to the last row
during the school's Annual Day practice,
the boy who brought Maggi in the lunchbox
every day,
the girlfriend who never chooses the restaurant,
movie, or food on dates,

the kid who still sits on the corner of the bed
when he is at someone's place,
the roommate who occupies the smaller space in
the cupboard, fridge, or other cabinets.

The middle benchers,
the spaces between words,
the little dots on my *Is* and soft dashes on my *Ts*,
the front-row theatre seats,
the in-betweeners,
the unbothered yellowish-orange afternoons of
people,
the unnamed planets,
the 7.5 IMDb ratings,
the beiges of humankind,
and other lukewarm thingamajigs.

I see you.
For I, too, think I am a child of mediocrity.

Problem of Plenty

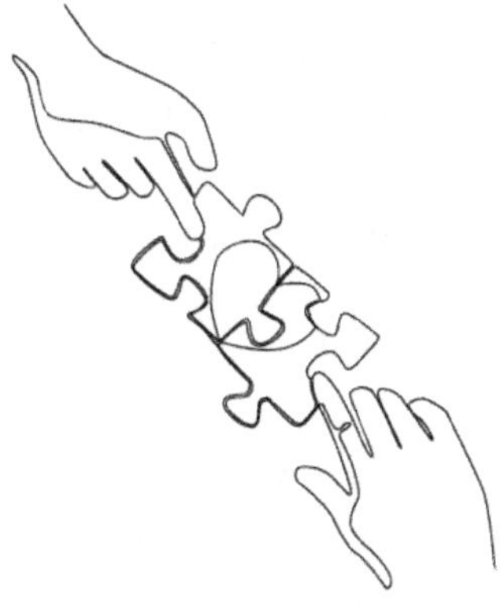

I love much.

I belong to the kind who can gift-wrap your
menial moments in one-liners or paragraphs,

who can smooth out all your frowns by kissing
your unloved places,

who can turn you into a fuzzy and warm
cupcake with a centre filled with molten love,

who can catch fireflies at night and bottle them
to light up your darkest parts,

who can pour you overflowing cups of love with
every morning tea of yours,

who can help you find joy in your rough days,
your handkerchief creases, and table drawers,

who can help you realise and wear the perfume
of your extraordinary personality everyday,

who can slip confetti of self-love in your pocket
everyday when you step out,

who can dissolve so much love in your life that
even if I leave you someday, you will feel the
warmth even after I am long gone.

But only if you love me right,
left, and centre.

Ode to Anxiety

I put my shirt buttons in the wrong order, twice;
my morning tea doesn't have enough tea (oh,
how I like it strong);
the insides of my cheeks are fully scraped
(overchewed);
got 3 unanswered calls on my phone;
my workplace seems much farther than it
usually is;
my feet are tapping incessantly in the most
non-rhythmic way;
I am using more hands than mouth while
talking;
my earphones seem tangled since 1972.
Don't call my name, you will find me startled.
I wish I was here, I wish I was here.

My intestines have tied themselves in a knot
again,

the bulbous mass rising, beating, taking shapes,
growing a vein,
slithering through my oesophagus, breaking and
churning the rib cage along the way.
The chalk quarry of my bones dissolves into my
bloodstream,
my mouth tastes like blood and iron, foaming.
Before it chokeholds the medulla,
I throw up.

It feels lighter, much lighter.
For now, at least.

Holding On

Some days, I am barely holding on:

like the fragile existence of a button sewn on a
shirt with a thin thread,

like poorly glued pieces of paper by a kid in his
art class,

like a tyre of a toy car held with a loose screw,

like a plucked flower soaked in water,

like an untamed hair coming out of the tightly
woven plait,

like a corn fallen out of a countryside truck and
lying on the road near a farm,

like an old dog sleeping away from a barn on a
breezy night,

like overly-dried clothes still hanging on the
rope,

like a mahogany door with rusty hinges,

like petals of a dry rose between the pages of an
old book,

like a half-broken toenail,

like an old couple in a loveless marriage.

Grace

I like how we...

put our hand out of the window to see how much
it is raining,

instantaneously touch the forehead of a close
person when we think they have a temperature,

taste the food we prepared before serving it to
our loved ones,

have that little smile on our face when we think
about the person we have a crush on,

put one leg or hand out of the blanket while
sleeping when we don't understand the weather,

want to pick up a flower when we see one lying
on the ground,

automatically bow our head a little every time
we pass a temple or mosque.

So much to love, so much to appreciate.

Freedom

But what is freedom exactly?

Is it releasing a bird caged by you and letting it go? Is it because you have caged it, you know freedom tastes better for him?

Or, is it the state of always being free—being born free and dying free, not even knowing how it feels to not be free?
Will you know the real taste, the real value of your freedom?

Or, is it the mixture, the day and night of freedom and unfreedom packed in a jar, shaken before use to know which side is effective and which is not?

How do you even decide, what is free and what
is not?

Does that woman walking on the road look as
free and safe to you as your sister at home
playing with her dog?
Or, does your sister look as safe and sound to
you as your wife when she is sleeping next to
you in your bed?

How do you even compare? How do you
decide?
And, most importantly, who are you to even
decide?

Finding You

I try to find you

in those bottles with shimmering drinks,

in glasses clinking on menial jokes,

in dance steps on loud music,

in corner seats of a movie hall,

in tables full of fancy hors d'oeuvres,

in smoke circles of a hukka,

in the steamy backseat of a car,

in long drives on long roads,

in sand-covered rocks near the sea,

in the blowing wind from the window seat of a
cab,

in bustling shopping streets,

in roadside shops with deep red kebabs hanging
on the skewers,

in crowded malls and elevators,

in forest side camps on a long weekend,

in muddy trekkings,

in the blue waters of fancy resorts,

in cutesy nail extensions and expensive spa
sessions,

in long star-gazing nights on the terrace,

in friendly tennis matches,

in rains, birthday parties, expensive clubs,

in whatnot, in whatnot.

Chan Kitthan

We wove a small tent with the material of the
nights in the wilds of Mumbai.

Made a bonfire with your LED screen and that
bright, oddly-shaped neon sign.

Filled the air inside with conversations about
music, politics, dark humour, and music again.
And lit it up with the fireflies of our phone
screens.

Meal was always dinner and meat was always
the choice for the wildlings like us—Jimis
Burger's ground beef patty and Chicken 65 on
Chicken 65 pizza is still meat, right?

Monsoon rains, Ali Sethi, Poets of the Fall, and
Hozier were perfect guests some nights

You asked how would I like to pay for all this
and I said 'For you, always in kind.'

Now, we have moved from camps to forts,
seven seas of emotions away.
Yet, somewhere Chan Kithan plays in the
background and I stop sometimes.

Words

I like how we find words in odd places:

on a scribbled window of a car after a dusty
night,

on the old cardboard boxes lying in a store
room,

on my mother's masala-stained dabbas,

on the stickers on deep maroons of imported
(supposedly) apples,

on the label of grandma's pashmina shawl,

on the steamy bathroom mirror after a long bath,

on musky, etched tins of old cold cream,

on a folded, papery-inky scented 100-rupee note,

on the palm of a lover's mehendi-laden hands,

on an old handkerchief bearing
hand-embroidered initials,

on half-crushed Starbucks cups with misspelt
names,

on those small rice pendants bought on the way
to Haji Ali,

on a lipstick-smeared crumpled tissue in an old
bag,

much like finding life, growing in crevices.

Abandonment

Things I abandoned during the last few years:

1. 19-season long series about medical drama
2. A small floral pouch for putting my makeup
3. Paragraphs about my unrequited love
4. Efforts of reconciliation with my father
5. My kitten who drowned in a well and died
6. Eighth-grade slambook
7. Conversations with a man I cherished the most
8. A stained bedsheet
9. Article about AI's role in changing our perception of life
10. A T-shirt I left to dry for too long

11. Stand-up notes about childhood trauma
12. A self-written book called '7 Ways to Happiness'
13. Also, a self-written book called 'Past Lovers'
14. Glass of Long Island Tea in a club
15. Eye contact with an out-of-my-league guy at a restaurant
16. A crushed brown paper bag from Blinkit in my room
17. Road to forgiveness leading to my mother
18. Recent assignment at work
19. Pair of earrings on a beach
20. Also, a pair of earrings at someone's place
21. A heavily embroidered dress in a mall
22. A part of me afraid to look into the mirror
23. My childhood

Burnt Oakwood

I looked at other girls, their skin like tulip petals,
perfectly stretched, delicately laid,
pressed against the features of their face.

Mine was oak wood.
Not the oakwood that adorns high-end floors,
but the oak tossed into the fireplace to burn.
Enough to light up the room for a while,
yet never turning to ashes.

I wish my mom had not put that wood in the
fireplace.
Or wait, why am I even in someone's fireplace?
If we're drawing parallels with a tree,

why am I at such an opposite end of the
spectrum where tulips bloom?
I am no flower, but am I not a leaf or at least a
branch?

Hmmm, a green, luscious leaf on a plant...
No, a withering leaf—
slightly brown, because the owner is in her 20s,
up late, always forgetting to water her plants on
the balcony...
No, but a golden brownish leaf has a rustic
charm...
No, I am a crisp brown leaf,
toasted in the sunlight. That's it...
no, wait...

"Hey, you—fourth bench, second girl with the
handkerchief in her hand."
I quickly looked to my left and right,
"Me, ma'am?"
"Yes, you. Pay attention in class."
She noticed I was still looking at the big diagram
on page 231,
while she read from page 234.
Absolutely mortified and muttered under my
breath,
"I am burnt oak wood, aren't I?"

Old Man in the Woods

What if I tell you that there is an old man living in the woods:

He watches birds from his window all day and marvels at his own creations.

His days are painted with the same bold strokes of comforting boredom.

He wakes up and makes himself a toast every morning. Every morning for the last 243 years.

He relishes the toast while reading the newspaper from the nearest town from where he gets the updates.

He mends the broken corner of his crooked bed
sometimes with an old hammer and some screws
from his toolbox.

Sometimes, he wanders off to the fields and
plucks juicy cherry tomatoes, green curry leaves,
or a trout from a small river nearby

He takes his old dog for a stroll in the evening.
They lazily sit on a trodden bench after a while.

He makes stew with his little wild vegetables on
his old stove at around 8.
He sleeps in his crooked bed embraced in the
sweet comfort of old age.

He can no longer watch over us or answer our
prayers.
Some days, he even forgets that he is God.
But, you would still worship him, right?

Reclamation

I am tired of moulding and bending my neck
muscles and jawbones into nods and yeses to
serve you.

I don't know how much of my flesh I have to
carefully stretch to properly fit into your ideas of
beauty:

I don't want to break my pieces and glue them
together in pretty shapes for the two sets of your
eyes to feast upon.

How many years of privilege did it take for you
to carefully suture these pieces of patriarchy into
a world with progressive little windows as token
gestures?

The small houses you have built with carefully crafted kitchens to fit my multi-dimensional personality, whose walls are now blackening with the soot of my ambitions.

Sure, with the little room that you assign me to spread my wings but not enough to overshadow your achievements.

I don't even need you to handle me the ammunition to blow up this suffocating emporium you have been building around me to stay in.

I am not your femme fatale. And there is no La Vie En Rose playing in the background.

This is not a cacophony to tear down the small cabinets that you have assigned me to store away my dreams for later years.

For this is a declaration of freedom from all the worldly things you want me to abide by but I simply refuse.

Sound of Death

What does death sound like?

'The flame is dying.'

'I can hear noises.'

'He is coming to take me.'

'The lights are going off.'

'My hair is being pulled.'

'Why is it so cold?'

'I feel nothing.'

Acknowledgements

This book would not have come to fruition without the support and encouragement of many remarkable individuals.

My mother, for her unwavering love and patience. And, for not asking what I am doing in my free time.

My brother, Dinesh, for being the anchor he has always been.

My father, for constantly radiating care and support.

Abhinav, for being the sounding board and an impeccable friend.
Sneha, for always being there and never giving up on me.

Finally, BookLeaf Publishing, for their steadfast belief in the project. Their guidance has been instrumental in bringing this book to life.

With sincere appreciation,
Deepti.